INDIANS

A Play

by Arthur Kopit

SAMUEL FRENCH, INC.
45 WEST 25TH STREET   NEW YORK 10010
7623 SUNSET BOULEVARD   HOLLYWOOD 90046
LONDON   *TORONTO*

IMPORTANT BILLING AND CREDIT REQUIREMENTS

All producers of INDIANS *must* give credit to the Author of the Play in all programs distributed in connection with performances of the Play and in all instances in which the title of the Play appears for purposes of advertising, publicizing or otherwise exploiting the Play and/or a production. The name of the Author *must* also appear on a separate line, on which no other name appears, immediately following the title, and *must* appear in size of type not less than fifty percent the size of the title type.

Acknowledgments

The idea for this play occurred to me in March, 1966. Since then, there have been many persons whose help has been instrumental in the play's reaching its final form: first, my producer, Lyn Austin, to whom I described its basic concept, and who gave me an advance of money so I could afford to research the necessary historical material; then, the wonderful actors and staff of the Royal Shakespeare Company, who presented the play some two years later, and especially Jack Gelber, who directed the excellent London production, and whose firsthand knowledge of the American Indians was constantly invaluable; Zelda Fitchandler and the staff and actors of the Arena Stage, where the next and greatly rewritten version of the play was produced, which afforded me still another relatively unstressful opportunity to view what I had written; Gene Frankel, who staged the Washington and New York productions and asked a seemingly endless number of incisive, important, and fundamental questions; my agent, Audrey Wood, who—with great affection—kept urging further rewrites, and who only smiled when I said I thought this enterprise threatened to become a lifelong task. I would particularly like to thank the Rockefeller Foundation, which gave me a grant of money so my wife and I could live in Europe during the time my play was in production there, and then allowed us to go, immediately after the production, to the fantastic Villa Serbelloni, at Lake Como, where the basic rethinking and fundamental reshaping of the play was done.

Indians was first performed by the Royal Shakespeare Company on July 4, 1968, at the Aldwych Theatre, London. Its American premiere was on May 6, 1969, at the Arena Stage, Washington, D. C.

Indians opened in New York at the Brooks Atkinson Theatre on October 13,1969, with the following cast:

BUFFALO BILL	Stacy Keach
SITTING BULL	Manu Tupou
SENATOR LOGAN	Tom Aldredge
SENATOR DAWES	Richard McKenzie
SENATOR MORGAN	Jon Richards
TRIAL SOLDIERS	Bob Hamilton
	Richard Nieves
JOHN GRASS	Sam Waterston
SPOTTED TAIL	James J. Sloyan
GRAND DUKE ALEXIS	Raul Julia
INTERPRETER	Yusef Bulos
NED BUNTLINE	Charles Durning
GERONIMO	Ed Rombola
MASTER VALET	Darryl Croxton
FIRST LADY	Dortha Duckworth
OL' TIME PRESIDENT	Peter MacLean
WILD BILL HICKOK	Barton Heyman
TESKANJAVILA	Dimitra Arliss
UNCAS	Raul Julia
WHITE HOUSE ORCHESTRA	Tony Posk
	Peter Rosenfelt
VALETS	Joseph Ragno, Richard Novello
	Brian Donohue
CHIEF JOSEPH	George Mitchell
ANNIE OAKLEY	Pamela Grey
JESSE JAMES	Ronny Cox
BILLY THE KID	Ed Rombola
PONCHO	Raul Julia

```
BARTENDER ...................... Brian Donohue
COWBOYS ....... Richard Nieves, Richard Miller
                    Clint Allmon, Bob Hamilton
COLONEL FORSYTH ............. Peter MacLean
LIEUTENANT .................... Richard Novello
REPORTERS ........ Ronny Cox, Brian Donohue
                    Darryl Croxton
CRAZY  HORSE..................... Dino Laudicina
HE-WHO-HEARS-THUNDER...Robert McLean
RED CLOUD ........................... Andy Torres
LITTLE HAWK ........................ Jay Fletcher
KIOKUK............................. Princeton Dean
SATANTA ............................... Ed Henkel
OLD TAZA........................... Michael Ebbin
BLACK HAWK..................... Kevin Conway
TECUMSEH....................... Pascual Vaquer
YELLOW CLOUD .................... Wesley Fata
KICKING BEAR ...................... Gary Weber
TOUCH-THE-CLOUDS ............. Peter DeMaio
HOWLING  WOLF.................. Ted Goodridge
WHITE  ANTELOPE.................. Tom Fletcher
LOW DOG .......................... Philip Arsenault
NAICHE.............................. Juan Antonio
INDIAN DRUMMERS .............. Leon Oxman
                    Allan Silverman
```

Director, Gene Frankel; Setting, Oliver Smith;
Lighting, Thomas Skelton; Costumes, Marjorie
Slaiman; Music, Richard Peaslee; Choreography,
Julie Arenal; Associate Producer, Steven Sinn;
Production Assistant, Binti Hoskins

Chronology for a Dreamer

1846 William F. Cody born in Le Claire, Iowa, on February 26.

1866 Geronimo surrenders.

1868 William Cody accepts employment to provide food for railroad workers; kills 4,280 buffaloes. Receives nickname "Buffalo Bill."

1869 *Buffalo Bill, the King of the Border Men,* a dime novel by Ned Buntline, makes Buffalo Bill a national hero.

1872 Expedition west in honor of Grand Duke Alexis of Russia, Buffalo Bill as guide.

1876 Battle at the Little Big Horn; Custer killed.

1877 Chief Joseph surrenders.

1878 Buffalo Bill plays himself in *Scouts of the Plains,* a play by Ned Buntline.

1879 Wild Bill Hickok joins Buffalo Bill on the stage.

1883 Sitting Bull surrenders, is sent to Standing Rock Reservation.

1883 "Buffalo Bill's Wild West Show" gives first performance, is great success.

1885 Sitting Bull allowed to join Wild West Show, tours with company for a year.

1886 United States Commission visits Standing Rock Reservation to investigate Indian grievances.

1890 Sitting Bull assassinated, December 15.
1890 Wounded Knee Massacre, December 25.

The play derives, in part, from this chronology but does not strictly adhere to it.—A.K.

Scene 1

Audience enters to stage with no curtain. HOUSELIGHTS dim. On stage: three large glass cases, one holding a larger-than-lifesize effigy of Buffalo Bill in fancy embroidered buckskin. One, an effigy of Sitting Bull dressed in simple buckskin or cloth, no headdress, little if any ornamentation. The last case contains some artifacts: a buffalo skull, a bloodstained Indian shirt, and an old rifle. The surrounding stage is dark. The cases are lit by SPOTLIGHTS from above. Strange MUSIC coming from all about. Sense of dislocation. The HOUSELIGHTS fade to dark. MUSIC up. LIGHTS on the cases slowly dim. Sound of WIND, soft at first. The cases glide into the shadowy distance and disappear. Eerie LIGHT now on stage; dim SPOTLIGHTS sweep the floor as if trying to locate something in space. Brief, distorted strains of Western American MUSIC. A VOICE reverberates from all about the theatre.

VOICE. Cody ... *Cody ... Cody! ... CODY!*

(One of the SPOTLIGHTS passes something: A MAN ON A HORSE. The SPOTLIGHT slowly retraces itself, picks up the horse and rider. THEY are in a far corner of the stage; THEY move in slow motion.
The other SPOTLIGHTS now move toward them, until all converge. At first, the LIGHT is dim. As THEY come toward us, it gets brighter. The man is BUFFALO BILL, dressed as in the museum case. The HORSE is a glorious white artificial stallion with wild, glowing

11

eyes. THEY approach slowly, their slow motion gradually becoming normal speed. Vague sound of CHEERING heard. MUSIC becoming rodeo-like. More identifiable. Then, slowly, from the floor, an open-framed oval fence rises and encloses them. The HORSE shies.

Tiny LIGHTS, strung beneath the top bar of the fence, glitter faintly. The SPOTLIGHTS—multicolored— begin to crisscross about the oval. Ghostly-pale Wild West Show BANNERS slowly descend. Then! It's a WILD WEST SHOW! Loud, brassy MUSIC!

LIGHTS blazing everywhere!

The HORSE rears. His RIDER whispers a few words, calms him.

Then, a great smile on his face, BUFFALO BILL begins to tour the ring, one hand lightly gripping the reins, the other proudly waving his big Stetson to the unseen surrounding crowd. Surely it is a great sight; the HORSE prances, struts, canters, dances to the music, leaps softly through the light, BUFFALO BILL effortlessly in control of the whole world, the universe; eternity.)

BUFFALO BILL. Yessir, BACK AGAIN! That triumphant brassy music, those familiar savage drums! Should o' known I couldn't stay away! Should o' known here's where I belong! The heat o' that ol' spotlight on my face. Yessir ... Should o' known here's where I belong.... *(HE takes a deep breath, closes his eyes, savors the air. A pause.)* Reminded o' somethin' tol' me once by General Custer. You remember him—one o' the great dumbass men in history. Not fer nothin' that he graduated last in his class at West Point! Anyways, we was out on the plains one day, when he turned t' me, with a kind o' far-off look in his eye, an' said, "Bill! If there is one thing a man must never

fear, it's makin' a personal comeback." *(HE chuckles.)*
Naturally, I—

VOICE. *(Softly.)* And now, to start ...

BUFFALO BILL. *(Startled.)* Hm?

VOICE. *And now to start.*

BUFFALO BILL. But I ... just ... got up here.

VOICE. I'm sorry; it's time to start.

BUFFALO BILL. Can't you *wait a second?* WHAT'S
THE RUSH? *WAIT A SECOND!* (Silence. *HE takes a
deep breath; quiets his horse down.)* I'm sorry. But if I
seem a trifle edgy to you, it's only 'cause I've just come
from a truly harrowing engagement; seems my ... manager,
a ... rather *ancient* gentleman, made a terrible *mistake* an'
booked me int' what turned out t' be a ghost town! Well! I
dunno what you folks know 'bout show business, but le'
me tell you, there is nothin' more depressin' than playin'
two-a-day in a goddam ghost town! *(HE chuckles.)*

*(INDIANS appear around the outside of the ring. The
    HORSE senses their presence and shies; BUFFALO
    BILL, as if realizing what it means, turns in terror.)*

VOICE. Bill.

BUFFALO BILL. But—

VOICE. It's *time. (Pause.)*

BUFFALO BILL. Be—before we start, I'd ... just like
to say—

VOICE. Bill!

(The INDIANS slowly approach.)

BUFFALO BILL.—*to say* that ... I am a fine man. And
anyone who says otherwise is *WRONG!*

VOICE. *(Softly.)* Bill, *it's time.*

BUFFALO BILL. My life is an open book; I'm not *ashamed* of its bein' looked at!

VOICE. *(Coaxing tone.)* Bill . . .

BUFFALO BILL. I'm sorry, this is very ... hard ... for me t' say. But I believe I ... am a ... hero ... *A GODDAM HERO!*

(Indian MUSIC. His HORSE rears wildly. LIGHTS change for next scene.)

Scene 2

(LIGHT up on SITTING BULL. He is dressed simply—no feathered headdress. It is winter.)

SITTING BULL. I am Sitting Bull! ... In the moon of the first snow-falling, in the year half my people died from hunger, the Great Father sent three wise men ... to investigate the conditions of our reservation, though we'd been promised he would come himself.

(LIGHTS up on SENATORS LOGAN, MORGAN, and DAWES; they are flanked by armed SOLDIERS. Opposite them, in a semicircle, are Sitting Bull's PEOPLE, all huddling in tattered blankets from the cold.)

SENATOR LOGAN. Indians! Please be assured that this committee has not come to punish you or take away any of your land but only to hear your grievances, determine if they are just, and if so, remedy them. For we, like the Great Father, wish only the best for our Indian children.

(The SENATORS spread out various legal documents.)

SITTING BULL. They were accompanied by my friend, William Cody ...

(Enter BUFFALO BILL, collar of his overcoat turned up for the wind.)

SITTING BULL. ... in whose Wild West Show I'd once appeared ...

(BUFFALO BILL greets a number of the Indians.)

SITTING BULL. ... in exchange for some food, a little clothing. And a beautiful horse that could do tricks.

SENATOR MORGAN. Colonel Cody has asked if he might say a few words before testimony begins.

SENATOR LOGAN. We would be honored.

BUFFALO BILL. *(To the Indians.)* My ... brothers. *(Pause.)* I know how disappointed you all must be that the Great Father isn't here; I apologize for having said I thought I could bring him. *(Pause.)* However! The three men I *have* brought are by far his most trusted personal representatives. And I promise that talking to them will be the same as ... *(Pause. Softly.)* ... talking to him. *(Long pause; HE rubs his eyes as if to soothe a headache.)* To ... Sitting Bull, then ... *(HE stares at Sitting Bull.)* ... I would like to say that I hope you can overlook your disappointment. And remember what is at *stake* here. And not get angry ... or too impatient. *(Pause.)* Also, I hope you will ask your people to speak with open hearts when talking to these men. And treat them with the same great respect I have always shown to you, for these men have come to *help* you and your people. And I am afraid they may be the only ones left now who can.

SITTING BULL. And though there were many among us who wanted to speak first: men like Red Cloud! And Little Hawk! And He-Who-Hears-Thunder! And Crazy Horse! Men who were great warriors, and had counted many coups! And been with us at the Little Big Horn when we *KILLED CUSTER!* ... *(Pause.)* I would not let them speak.... For they were like me, and tended to get angry, easily. *(Pause.)* Instead, I asked the *young* man, John Grass, who had never fought at all, but had been to the white man's school at Carlisle, and *thought* he understood ... something ... of their ways.

BUFFALO BILL. Sitting Bull would like John Grass to speak first.

LOGAN. Call John Grass.

BUFFALO BILL. John Grass! Come forward.

(Enter JOHN GRASS in a black cutaway many sizes too small for him. He wears an Indian shirt. Around his neck is a medal.)

JOHN GRASS. *Brothers!* I am going to talk about what the Great Father told us a long time ago. He told us to give up hunting and start farming. So we did as he said, and our people grew hungry. For the land was suited to grazing not farming, and even if we'd been farmers, nothing could have grown. So the Great Father said he would send us food and clothing, but nothing came of it. So we asked him for the money he had promised us when we sold him the Black Hills, thinking, with this money we could *buy* food and clothing. But nothing came of it. So we grew ill and sad.... So to help us from this sadness, he sent Bishop Marty to teach us to be Christians. But when we told him we did not wish to be Christians but wished to be like our

fathers, and dance the sundance, and fight bravely against
the Shawnee and the Crow!—and pray to the Great Spirits
who made the four winds, and the earth, and made man
from the dust of this earth, Bishop Marty hit us! ... So we
said to the Great Father that we thought we would like to
go *back* to hunting, because to live, we needed food. But
we found that while we had been learning to farm, the
buffalo had gone away. And the plains were filled now only
with their bones. ...Before we give you any more of our
land, or move from here where the people we loved are
growing white in their coffins, we want you to tell the
Great Father to give us, who still live, what he promised
he would! *No more than that.*

SITTING BULL. I prayed for the return of the buffalo!
*(LIGHTS fade to black on everyone but BUFFALO BILL.
Distant GUNSHOT heard offstage. Pause. Two more
GUNSHOTS. LIGHTS to black on BUFFALO BILL.)*

Scene 3

*(LIGHT up on SPOTTED TAIL, standing on a ledge above
the plains. It is night, and he is lit by a pale MOON.
The air is hot. No wind. A rifle SHOT is heard offstage,
of much greater presence than the previous shots.
SPOTTED TAIL peers in its direction. Sound, offstage,
of WOUNDED BULLS. Enter an INDIAN dressed as a
buffalo, wounded in the eye and bellowing with pain.
HE circles the stage. Enter two more BUFFALOES,
also wounded in the eyes. The first BUFFALO dies.
The two other BUFFALOES stagger over to his side
and die beside him; another BUFFALO [missing an eye]
enters, staggers in a circle, senses the location of the
dead buffaloes and heads dizzily toward them—dying en*

*route, halfway there. SPOTTED TAIL crouches and
gazes down at them. Then HE stares up at the sky.
NIGHT CREATURES screech in the dark. A pause)*

BUFFALO BILL. (*Offstage but coming closer.*) Ninety-
three, ninety-four, ninety-five ... ninety-six! I DID IT!

*(Enter, running, a much younger BUFFALO BILL, rifle in
hand, followed shortly by MEMBERS OF THE U.S.
CAVALRY bearing torches, and the GRAND DUKE'S
INTERPRETER.)*

BUFFALO BILL. I did it, I did it! No one believed I
could, but *I did it*! One hundred buffalo—one hundred
shots! "You jus' gimme some torches," I said. "I *know*
there's buffalo around us. *Here*. Put yer ear t' the ground.
Feel it tremblin'? Well. You wanna see somethin' fantastic,
you get me some torches. I'll shoot the reflections in their
eyes. I'll shoot 'em like they was so many shiny nickels!"
INTERPRETER. I'll tell the Grand Duke you did what
you said. I know he'll be pleased.
BUFFALO BILL. Well he oughta be! I don' give
exhibitions like this fer just anybody!

(Exit the INTERPRETER.)

BUFFALO BILL. 'Specially as these critters 're gettin'
so damn hard t' find. (*To the soldiers.*) Not like the ol' days
when I was huntin' 'em fer the railroads. (*HE laughs, gazes
down at one of the buffaloes. Pause. HE looks away;
squints as if in pain.*)
A SOLDIER. Are you all right, sir?
BUFFALO BILL. Uh ... Yes. Fine.

(Exit the SOLDIERS.

BUFFALO BILL rubs his head.
SPOTTED TAIL hops down from his perch and walks up
    behind Cody unnoticed; stares at him. Pause.
BUFFALO BILL senses the Indian's presence and turns,
    cocking his rifle. The INDIAN makes no move.
BUFFALO BILL stares at the Indian. Pause.)

BUFFALO BILL. *Spotted Tail!* My God. I haven't seen you in years. How ... ya been? *(Slight laugh.)*
    SPOTTED TAIL. *What are you doing here*?

(Pause.)

BUFFALO BILL. Well, well what ... are *you* doing here? This isn't Sioux territory!
    SPOTTED TAIL. It isn't *your* territory either.

(Pause.)

BUFFALO BILL. Well I'm with ... these *people*. I'm scoutin' for 'em.
    SPOTTED TAIL. *These people* ... must be very hungry.
    BUFFALO BILL. Hm?
    SPOTTED TAIL. To need so many buffalo.
    BUFFALO BILL. Ah! Of course! You were following the buffalo *also*! ... Well listen, I'm sure my friends won't mind you takin' some. 'Tween us, my friends don't 'specially care for the *taste* o' buffalo meat. *(HE laughs.)* My God, but it's good t' see you again!
    SPOTTED TAIL. *Your friends: I* have been studying them from the hills. They are very strange. They seem neither men, nor women.
    BUFFALO BILL. Well! Actually, they're sort of a new *breed* o' people. Called dudes. *(HE chuckles.)*

SPOTTED TAIL. You *like* them?

BUFFALO BILL. Well ... sure. Why not? *(Pause.)* I mean, obviously, they ain't the sort I've been used to. But then, things're changin' out here. An' these men are the ones who're changin' 'em. So, if you wanna be *part* o' these things, an' not left behind somewhere, you jus' plain hafta get *used* to 'em. You—uh—follow ... what I mean? *(Silence.)* I mean ... you've got to *adjust*. To the times. Make a *plan* fer yerself. I have one. You should have one, too. Fer yer own good. Believe me. *(Long pause.)*

SPOTTED TAIL. *What is your plan?*

BUFFALO BILL. Well, my plan is t' help people. Like you, ferinstance. Or these people I'm with. More ... even ... than that, maybe. And, and, whatever ... it is I *do* t' help, for it, these people may someday jus' possibly name streets after me. Cities. Counties. States! I'll ... be as famous as Dan'l Boone! ... An' somewhere, on top of a beautiful mountain that overlooks more plains 'n rivers than any other mountain, there might even be a statue of me sittin' on a great white horse, a-wavin' my hat t' everyone down below, thankin' 'em, fer thankin' me, fer havin' done ... whatever ... it is I'm gonna ... *do* fer 'em all. How come you got such a weird look on yer face?

BUNTLINE. *(Offstage.)* HEY, CODY! *STAY WHERE YA ARE!*

BUFFALO BILL. DON' WORRY! I AIN'T BUDGIN'! *(To Spotted Tail.)* That's Mister Ned Buntline, the well-known newspaper reporter. I think he's gonna do an *article* on me! General Custer, who's in charge, an' I think is pushin' fer an article on *himself*, says this may well be the most important western expedition since Lewis 'n Clark.

BUNTLINE. *(Offstage.)* BY THE WAY, *WHERE* ARE YA?

BUFFALO BILL. I ... AIN'T SURE! JUST HEAD FOR THE LIGHTS! *(HE laughs to himself.)*

SPOTTED. TAIL. Tell me. Who is the man everyone always bows to?

BUFFALO BILL. Oh! The Gran' Duke! He's from a place called Russia. This whole shindig's in his honor. I'm sure he'd love t' meet you. He's never seen a real Indian.

SPOTTED TAIL. There are no Indians in Russia?

(BUFFALO BILL shakes his head.)

SPOTTED TAIL. Then I will study him even more carefully than the others. Maybe if he takes me back to Russia with him, I will not end like my people will end.

BUFFALO BILL. *(Startled.) What?*

SPOTTED TAIL. I mean, like these fools here, on the ground. *(HE stares at the buffalo.)*

BUFFALO BILL. Ah ... Well, if ya don' mind my sayin', I think you're bein' a bit pessimistic. But you do what ya like. Jus' remember: these people you're studyin'— some folk think *they're* the fools.

SPOTTED TAIL. Oh, no! They are not fools! *No one who is a white man can be a fool. (HE smiles coldly at Buffalo Bill.)*

(Heraldic Russian FANFARE offstage.
Enter RUSSIAN TORCHBEARERS and TRUM-
PETEERS.
BUFFALO BILL and SPOTTED TAIL, in awe, back
away.
Enter with much pomp and ceremony GRAND DUKE
ALEXIS on a splendid litter carved like a horse. HE is
accompanied by his INTERPRETER, who points out
the four buffaloes to the Grand Duke as HE majestically
circles the clearing. HE is followed by NED
BUNTLINE, who carries a camera and tripod.)

BUFFALO BILL. My God, but that is a beautiful sight!

(The GRAND DUKE comes to a halt. Majestic sweep of his arms to those around him. GRAND DUKE makes a regal Russian speech.)

INTERPRETER. His Excellency the Grand Duke wishes to express his heartfelt admiration of Buffalo Bill ...

(MUSIC up.)

INTERPRETER. ... for having done what he has done tonight.

(The GRAND DUKE gestures majestically. The INTERPRETER opens a small velvet box. Airy MUSIC. The INTERPRETER walks toward Buffalo Bill.)

GRAND DUKE. *(Gesturing for Buffalo Bill to come forward.)* Boofilo Beel!

*(BUFFALO BILL walks solemnly forward. The INTERPRETER takes out a medal. BUFFALO BILL, deeply moved, looks around, embarrassed. The INTERPRETER smiles and holds up the medal, gestures warmly for Buffalo Bill to kneel. HE does so. The INTERPRETER places the medal, which is on a bright ribbon, around his neck.
FLASHGUN goes off.)*

BUNTLINE. Great picture, Cody! FRONT PAGE! My God, what a night! *What a story!* Uh ... sorry, yer

Highness. Didn't mean t' disturb ya. (*HE backs meekly away. Sets up his camera for another shot.*)

(*The GRAND DUKE regains his composure. GRAND DUKE performs a Russian speech.*)

INTERPRETER. His Excellency wonders how Buffalo Bill became such a deadly shot.
BUFFALO BILL. Oh, well, you know, just ... practice. (*Embarrassed laugh.*)

(*GRAND DUKE performs a Russian speech.*)

INTERPRETER. His Excellency says he wishes that his stupid army knew how to practice.

(*GRAND DUKE: Russian speech.*)

INTERPRETER. Better yet, he wishes you would come back with him to his palace and protect him yourself.
BUFFALO BILL. Oh. (*Slight laugh.*) Well, I'm sure the Grand Duke's in excellent hands.

(*The INTERPRETER whispers what Buffalo Bill has just said.*)

GRAND DUKE. Da! Hands. (*HE holds out his hands, then turns them and puts them around his throat.*)
BUFFALO BILL. I think His Majesty's exaggeratin'. I can't believe he's not surrounded by friends.
GRAND DUKE. FRIENDS! (*HE cackles and draws his sword, slashes the air.*) Friends! Friends! ... Friends! (*HE fights them off.*)
BUFFALO BILL. (*To Buntline.*) I think he's worried 'bout somethin'.

BUNTLINE. Very strange behavior.

(GRAND DUKE: nervous Russian speech.)

INTERPRETER. His Excellency wonders if Buffalo Bill has ever been afraid.
BUFFALO BILL. ... Afraid?

(GRAND DUKE: Russian word.)

INTERPRETER. Outnumbered.
BUFFALO BILL. Ah. *(Slight laugh.)* Well, uh ...
BUNTLINE. Go on, tell 'm. It'll help what I'm planin' t' write.
BUFFALO BILL. *(Delighted.)* It *will*?
BUNTLINE. Absolutely. Look: the West is changin'— right? Well, people wanna know about it. Wanna feel ... *part* o' things. I think *you're* what they need. Someone t' listen to, observe, *identify* with. No, no, really! I been studyin' you.
BUFFALO BILL. ... You have?
BUNTLINE. I think you could be the inspiration o' this land.
BUFFALO BILL. Now I *know* you're foolin'!
BUNTLINE. Not at all.... Well go on. Tell 'm what he wants t' hear. Through my magic pen, others will hear also.... Donmentionit. The nation needs men like me, too. *(HE pats Cody on the shoulder and shoves him off toward the Grand Duke.)*

(CODY gathers his courage.)

BUFFALO BILL. *(To the Grand Duke.)* Well, uh .. where can I begin? Certainly it's true that I've been outnumbered. And—uh—many times. Yes.

BUNTLINE. That's the way.

BUFFALO BILL. More times, in fact, than I can count.

BUNTLINE. Terrific.

BUFFALO BILL. *(Warming to the occasion.)* An' believe me, I can count pretty high!

BUNTLINE. SENSATIONAL!

BUFFALO BILL. Mind you, 'gainst *me*, twelve's normally an even battle—long's I got my two six-shooters that is.

BUNTLINE. Keep it up, keep it up!

BUFFALO BILL. THIRTEEN! If one of 'em's thin enough for a bullet t' go clean through. Fourteen if I got a huntin' knife. Fifteen if there's a hard surface off o' which I can ricochet a few shots.

BUNTLINE. *Go on!*

BUFFALO BILL. Um, twenty ... if I got a stick o' dynamite. HUNDRED! IF THERE'S ROCKS T' START A AVALANCHE!

(BUNTLINE applauds.)

BUFFALO BILL. What I mean is, with *me* it's never say die! Why ... I remember once I was ridin' for the Pony Express 'tween Laramie 'n Tombstone. Suddenly, jus' past the Pecos, fifty drunk Comanches attack. Noise like a barroom whoop-di-do, arrows fallin' like hailstones! I mean, they come on me so fast they don' have time t' see my face, notice who I am, realize I'm in fact a very good *friend o'* theirs!

GRAND DUKE. FRIEND! FRIEND!

BUNTLINE. *(Sotto voce.)* Get off the subject!

BUFFALO BILL. Well, there was no alternative but t' fire back. Well I'd knocked off 'bout thirty o' their number when I realized I was *out* o' bullets. Just at that moment, a arrow whizzed past my head. Thinkin' fast, I reached out an' caught it. Then, usin' it like a fly swatter, I knocked away the other nineteen arrows that were headin' fer my heart. Whereupon, I stood up in the stirrups, hurled the arrow sixty yards ... An' killed their chief. *(Pause.)* Which ... *depressed* ... the remainin' Indians. *(Pause.)* And sent 'em scurryin' home. Well! That's sort o' what ya might call a typical day!

(Bravos from everyone except the GRAND DUKE.
GRAND DUKE: Russian speech, quite angry.)

INTERPRETER. His Excellency says he would like to kill a Comanche also.
BUFFALO BILL. Hm?
GRAND DUKE. *(With obvious jealousy.)* Like Boofilo Beel!
INTERPRETER. Like Buffalo Bill!

(GRAND DUKE: excited Russian speech.)

INTERPRETER. He will *prove* he cannot be intimidated!
GRAND DUKE. Rifle, rifle, rifle!
BUFFALO BILL. *(To Buntline.)* I think my story may've worked a bit too well.
BUNTLINE. Nonsense! This is *terrific!*

(THEY duck as the GRAND DUKE, cackling madly, scans the surrounding darkness over his rifle sight.)

BUNTLINE. Shows you've won the Grand Duke's heart.
GRAND DUKE. *(Pounding his chest.)* Boofilo Beel! I ... am *BOOFILO BEEL! (HE laughs demonically.)*
BUNTLINE. I think you'd better find 'm a Comanche.

BUFFALO BILL. Right! *Well.* Um ... *(Slight laugh.)*
That *could* be a ... problem.

GRAND DUKE. Comanche! *Comanche!*

BUFFALO BILL. Ya see, fer one thing, the Comanches
live in Texas. And we're in Missouri.

GRAND DUKE. COMANCHE! *COMANCHE!*

BUFFALO BILL. Fer another, I ain't 'xactly sure what
they look like.

GRAND DUKE. Ah!

*(HE fires into the darkness. SPOTTED TAIL stumbles
out, collapses and dies. The GRAND DUKE and his
INTERPRETER delirious with joy. BUNTLINE
dumfounded. BUFFALO BILL stunned, but for vastly
different reasons.)*

BUNTLINE. *(Approaching the body cautiously.)* My
God, will you look at that? Fate must be smiling! *(HE
laughs weakly, stares up at the heavens in awe.)*

*(BUFFALO BILL, almost in a trance, walks over to the
body; stares down at it. Weird MUSIC heard. The
LIGHTS change color, grow vague. All movement
arrested. SPOTTED TAIL rises slowly and moves just
as slowly toward the Grand Duke; stops.)*

SPOTTED TAIL. My name is Spotted Tail. My father
was a Sioux; my mother, part Cherokee, part Crow. No
matter how you look at it, I'm just not a Comanche. *(HE
sinks back to the ground. LIGHTS return to normal, the
MUSIC ends.)*

(GRAND DUKE: baffled Russian speech.)

INTERPRETER. His Excellency would like to know what the man he just shot has said.

(Long pause. BUFFALO BILL looks around, as if for help; ALL EYES upon him.)

BUFFALO BILL. *(Softly.)* He said ... *(Pause.)* "I ... *(Pause.)* should have ... *(HE looks at Buntline takes a deep breath.)* stayed at home in ... Texas with the rest of my ... Comanche tribe."

BUNTLINE. Fabulous! *(HE takes Spotted Tail's picture; the night sky GLOWS from the flash.)* Absolutely fabulous!

(The scene fades around BUFFALO BILL, who stands in the center, dizzily gripping his head.)

Scene 4

(Dimly we see the SENATORS and SITTING BULLS' INDIANS glide back into view.)

BUFFALO BILL. If it *please* the honorable senators ... there is something I would like to say to *them*, as well. *(Pause.)* I wish to say ... that there is far more at stake here today than the discovery of Indian grievances. *(Pause.)* At stake are these people's lives. In *some* ways, more than even that. For these are not just *any* Indians. These are *Sitting Bull's* Indians ... The last to surrender. The last of a kind. So, in that way, you see, they are ... perhaps more *important* for us than ... any others. For it is we, alone, who have put them on this strip of arid land. And what becomes of them is ... our responsibility. *(BUFFALO*

BILL stares helplessly as the scene about him fades to black.)
VOICE. And now, for your *pleasure*, BUFFALO BILL'S WILD WEST SHOW *PROUDLY* PRESENTS ...

(LIGHTS to black. DRUM ROLL.)

Scene 5

(Stage dark; DRUM ROLL continues. Weirdly colored SPOTLIGHTS begin to crisscross on the empty stage.)

VOICE. THE MOST FEROCIOUS INDIAN ALIVE!

(The bars of a large round cage slowly emerge from the floor of the stage; then, around the bars, the Wild West Show fence seen earlier.)

VOICE. THE FORMER SCOURGE OF THE SOUTHWEST! ...

(The LIGHTS on the fence begin to glow; eerie, fantastical atmosphere. A tunnel-cage rolls out from the wings and connects with the large central cage. Sound of an IRON GRATE opening offstage. Rodeo MUSIC up.)

VOICE. ... The one 'n only ... *GERONIMO*!

(Enter GERONIMO, crawling through the tunnel; as soon as he is in sight, HE stops, lifts his head, takes in his surroundings. Enter two COWBOY ROUSTABOUTS with prods. THEY are enormous men—much larger than life-size. Their muscles bulge against their gaudy

clothes. Their faces seem frozen in a sneer. Even their gun belts are oversized. They prod GERONIMO along, raise the gate to the center cage and coax him in, closing it behind him. Then THEY move away.)

(GERONIMO paces about, testing the bars with his hands.)

GERONIMO. I AM GERONIMO! WAR CHIEF OF THE GREAT CHIRICAHUA APACHES! *(HE stalks about.)* Around my neck is a string of white men's genitals! MEN I HAVE KILLED! Around my waist, the scalplocks of white women's genitals! WOMEN I RAPED AND KILLED! *No Indian has ever killed or raped more than I*! Even the Great Spirits cannot count the number!.My body is painted with blood! I am red from white men's BLOOD! NO ONE LIVES WHO HAS KILLED MORE WHITE MEN THAN *I*!

(BUFFALO BILL, in his fancy buckskin, enters unnoticed by GERONIMO; DRUM ROLL. HE opens the cage door and walks inside. Once inside, HE closes the door and stands still. GERONIMO senses his presence and stops moving. Lifts up his head as if to hear better. Sniffs. Turns. Stares at Buffalo Bill. Slowly, BUFFALO BILL walks toward him. HE stops just short of the Indian, then defiantly turns his back. GERONIMO practically frothing.
Long pause. GERONIMO does nothing.
BUFFALO BILL walks calmly away, opens the cage door, and exits. Disappears into the shadows. GERONIMO stands trembling with frenzy. LIGHTS fade to black.)

Scene 6

(LIGHTS up on the SENATE COMMITTEE, SITTING BULL'S INDIANS, and BUFFALO BILL.)

SENATOR LOGAN. Mister Grass, I wonder if you could be a bit more specific and tell us *exactly* what you think the Great Father has promised which he has not given.

JOHN GRASS. He promised to give us *as much as we would need, for as long as we would need it*!

SENATOR DAWES. Where did he promise you *that*?

JOHN GRASS. In a treaty.

SENATOR LOGAN. *What* treaty?

JOHN GRASS. A treaty signed some years ago, maybe five or six.

SENATOR LOGAN. Mister Grass, many treaties were signed five or six years ago. But frankly, I've never heard of an arrangement quite like that one.

JOHN GRASS. You took the Black Hills from us in this treaty!

SENATOR DAWES. You mean we *bought* the Black Hills in it!

(LOGAN glares at Dawes.)

JOHN GRASS. I have nothing else to say. *(HE turns and starts to walk away.)*

SENATOR LOGAN. Mister Grass! The Senator *apologizes* for his tone.

(Pause.)

JOHN GRASS. *(Returns.)* If you *bought* the Black Hills from us, where is our money?

SENATOR LOGAN. The money is in trust.

JOHN GRASS. *Trust*?

SENATOR MORGAN. He means, it's in a bank. Being *held* for you in a ... bank. In Washington! Very fine bank.

JOHN GRASS. Well, we would rather hold it ourselves.

SENATOR DAWES. The Great Father is worried that you've not been educated enough to spend it *wisely*. When he feels you have, you will receive every last penny of it. *Plus interest.*

(JOHN GRASS turns in fury; LOGAN totally exasperated with Dawes.)

BUFFALO BILL. Mister Grass, *please*! These men have come to *help* you! But their ways are *different* from yours; you must be *patient* with them.

JOHN GRASS. You said you would bring us the Great Father.

BUFFALO BILL. *I tried! I told* you! But he wouldn't come; *what else could I do*?

JOHN GRASS. You told us he was your *friend.*

BUFFALO BILL. HE *IS* MY FRIEND! *Look, don't you understand*? These men are your *only hope.* If you turn away from them, it's like *committing suicide.*

JOHN GRASS. *(Pause. To the Senators.)* At Fort Laramie, Fort Lyon, and Fort Rice we signed treaties, parts of which have never been fulfilled.

SENATOR DAWES. *Which* parts have never been fulfilled?

JOHN GRASS. At Fort Rice the Government advised us to be at peace, and said that if we did so, we would receive a span of horses, five bulls, ten chickens and a wagon!

SENATOR LOGAN. You really believe these things were in the treaty?

JOHN GRASS. We were told they were.

SENATOR LOGAN. You saw them written?

JOHN GRASS. We cannot read very well, but we were *told* they were!

(*The SENATORS glance sadly at one another. JOHN GRASS grows confused. Pause.*)

JOHN GRASS. We were also promised a steamboat!

SENATOR MORGAN. A *steamboat*?

SENATOR DAWES. What in God's name were you supposed to do with a steamboat in the middle of the plains? (*HE laughs.*)

JOHN GRASS. I don't know. (*HE turns in confusion and stares at Buffalo Bill.*)

(*BUFFALO BILL turns helplessly to the Senators as LIGHTS begins to fade.*)

SITTING BULL. Where is the Great Father, Cody? The one you said would help us. The one you said you knew *so well.*

(*As the LIGHTS go to black a MOZART minuet is heard.*)

Scene 7

LIGHTS up on White House Ballroom, in the center of which is a makeshift stage. The front drop of this stage is a melodramatic western-heroic poster with "Scouts of the Plains, by Ned Buntline" painted over it.

The MOZART stops as—A Negro USHER enters.)

    USHER. This way, Mister President.
    OL' TIME PRESIDENT. (*Offstage.*) Thank you.
George.

*(Enter the OL' TIME PRESIDENT in white tie and tails,
    cigar in mouth, brandy glass in hand.)*

    OL' TIME PRESIDENT. This way, dear. They're about
to start.
    FIRST LADY. (*Enters in a formal gown.*) Oh, it *is*
exciting. Our *first real cowboys!*

*(The USHER leads them toward a par of Louis XIV chairs
    set facing the stage. DRUM ROLL.)*

    OL' TIME PRESIDENT. Sssh. Here we go.

*(THEY sit. Enter from behind the canvas drop. NED
    BUNTLINE. HE wears an exaggerated version of a
    plainsman's outfit.)*

    NED BUNTLINE.
Mister President, hon'rable First Lady,
Before you stands a character most shady,
A knave whose presence darkens this bright earth,
More than does the moon's eclipsing girth. What's that
    you say, I'm rude to filth espouse,
When I'm the guest of such a clean, white house?
Fear not, there's somethin' I didn't mention:
Recently, I found redemption.
Ah, forgive me, I'm sorry, Ned Buntline's the name,
It's me who's brought Bill Cody fame.
Wrote twenty-seven books with him the hero,

Made 'm better known than Nero.
And though we sold 'em cheap, one for a dime,
The two of us was rich in no time.
As for my soul's redemption, it came thus:
I saw the nation profit more than us.
For with each one o' my excitin' stories,
Cody grew t' represent its glories.
Also helped relieve its conscience,
By showing pessimism's nonsense.
Later, when people asked t' *see* 'm,
I wrote a play for him to be in;
A scene of which we now perform for you,
As you've so graciously implored us to.
Cody, of course, impersonates himself,
As does Yours Truly.
The Crow maiden is Italian actress
Paula Monduli.
Our evil Pawnee Chief, the great German actor
Gunther Hookman.
Our other Indians, I'm afraid,
Come from Brooklyn.
However, as a special treat tonight,
A visitor is here,
And I've added some new dialogue,
So he might appear.
Realize though, this man's come as Cody's friend,
He's not an actor,
Though of course in *my* play, who men *are*
Is the real factor.
So get set then for anything,
May the script be damned,
An' let's give Cody an' Wild Bill Hickok
A ROUSING HAND!

*(The FIRST LADY and the OL' TIME PRESIDENT
applaud enthusiastically. BUNTLINE exits.*

*The canvas drop is rolled up to reveal another canvas
drop—a painted forest of the worst melodramatic order.*

*On stage, wooden as only the worst amateur actors can be,
stand CODY and HICKOK, the latter with long,
glorious hair, fancy buckskin leggings, two large guns
and a knife in his belt.)*

BUFFALO BILL. God pray we're in time. Those
Pawnee devils will do anything.

(Silence.)

BUNTLINE. *(Prompting from offstage.)* Especially ...

(Silence.)

BUFFALO BILL. Think that's your line, Bill.
WILD BILL HICKOK. Oh, hell's thunder. *(To
Buntline.)* Better give it-a-me agin.
BUNTLINE. Especially ...
WILD BILL HICKOK. Especially.
BUNTLINE. ... at their ...
WILD BILL HICKOK. At their.
BUFFALO BILL. *(Sotto voce.)* ... dreadful annual ...
WILD BILL HICKOK. Dreadful. Annual.
BUNTLINE. ... Festival of the Moon.
WILD BILL HICKOK. Festival of the Moon. Which is
...'bout t' happen. As it does every ...

(Silence.)

BUFFALO BILL. ... year.
WILD BILL HICKOK. Year.

BUNTLINE. Very good.

WILD BILL HICKOK. Very good.

BUNTLINE. No!

WILD BILL HICKOK. Whose line's that?

BUFFALO BILL. No one's. He was jus' congratulatin' you.

WILD BILL HICKOK. Oh, Will, fer pitty's sake, le' me out o' this.

BUNTLINE. *Ad lib!*

BUFFALO BILL. Yes! Pray God we're in time to stop the Pawnee's dreadful Festival of the Moon so that I, the great Buffalo Bill, can once again—

WILD BILL HICKOK. Will, stop it! A man may need money, but no man needs it this bad.

(*Enter BUNTLINE, tap-dancing the sound of horse's hooves.*)

BUFFALO BILL. Hark! Ned Buntline approaches! One o' the finest sharpshooters o' the West!

WILD BILL HICKOK. (*Under this breath.*) Couldn't hit a cow in the ass from two paces.

BUFFALO BILL. Who knows? Maybe *he* can help us in our dire strait.

WILD BILL HICKOK. Mister and Missus President, if you're still out there, believe me, I'm as plumb embarrassed by this dude-written sissyshit as you.

BUNTLINE. HAIL, BUFFALO BILL! Hail—uh—Wild Bill Hickok. What brings you to this unlikely place?

WILD BILL HICKOK. Good fuckin' question.

BUNTLINE. Could it be that you seek, as I do, the camp of Uncas, evil Pawnee chief?

BUFFALO BILL. Yes, verily. We seek his camp so that I, the great Buffalo Bill, can, once again, save someone in distress. (*HICKOK groans.*) This time, specifically, a virgin maiden—

WILD BILL HICKOK. You gotta be jokin'.

BUFFALO BILL. *Will you shut up!*—named Teskanjavila! Who, 'less I save her, faces torture, sacrifice, and certain violations.

BUNTLINE. This bein' so, *let us join forces*!

WILD BILL HICKOK. Boy, where's your *self-respect*?

BUNTLINE. (*Weakly.*) And save this virgin together.

BUFFALO BILL. (*To Hickok.*) Will you leave me alone!

WILD BILL HICKOK. This ain't a *proper place* for a man t' be!

BUFFALO BILL. Well, I THINK IT *IS*! I think I'm doin' a lot o' good up here! Entertainin' people! Makin 'em happy! Showin' 'em the West! Givin' 'em somethin' t' be *proud* of! *You* go spend your life in Dodge City if you want! I got *bigger* things in mind!

(*Stunned pause.*)

BUNTLINE. (*Very sheepishly.*) To repeat: let us join forces and save this virgin together.

WILD BILL HICKOK. Buntline, if these guns were loaded, I'd—

BUNTLINE. (*Cueing the actors offstage.*) HARK! The maiden's name is called!

NUMEROUS VOICES. (*Offstage.*) Teskanjavila!

BUNTLINE. We must be near the camp of Uncas.

BUFFALO BILL. Evil Pawnee chief.

WILD BILL HICKOK. I'm gettin' sick.

BUNTLINE. Let us, therefore, approach with caution.

BUFFALO BILL. Guns ready.

BUNTLINE. Ears open.

BUFFALO BILL. (*To Hickok.*) Mouths shut!

BUNTLINE. Eyes alert.

BUFFALO BILL. So that I, the great Buffalo Bill, may once aga—

(*HICKOK has walked over and is staring into his face.*)

BUFFALO BILL. Just *what are you doin'*?

WILD BILL HICKOK. What're *you* doin'?

BUFFALO BILL. I'm doin' what I'm doin', *that's* what I'm doin'!

WILD BILL HICKOK. (*To Buntline.*) Always was intelligent.

BUFFALO BILL. I am doin' what my country *wants*! WHAT MY BELOVED COUNTRY *WANTS*!

WILD BILL HICKOK. (*To First Family.*) *This* ... is ... what you want?

FIRST LADY. Absolutely!

OL' TIME PRESIDENT. Best play I've seen in years!

(*HICKOK, staggered, sits down on the stage.*)

BUFFALO BILL. When a man has a talent, a *God* given talent, I think it's his godly duty t'make the most of it.

(*APPLAUSE from FIRST FAMILY.*)

BUFFALO BILL. (*Nods acknowledgment. To Hickok.*) Ya see, Bill, what you fail to understand is that I'm not being false to what I *was*. I'm simply *drawin'* on what I was ... and raisin' it to a higher level. (*HE takes a conscious pause.*) *Now*. On with the show! (*HE points to Buntline, cueing him to give the next line.*)

BUNTLINE. AVAST, AHOY! Above yon trees see the pale moon rising!

(*A cardboard MOON is pulled upwards.*)

BUNTLINE. Feel the black night envelop us like a dark dream.

(*BUNTLINE and CODY shiver.*)

BUNTLINE. Sounds of the savage forest are heard.... We approach on tiptoes.
BUFFALO BILL. (*To the First Family.*) God pray we're in time.

(*THEY drop to their bellies as the canvas drop is raised to reveal the camp of Uncas. Tied to a totem pole is TESKANJAVILA, writing sensually.*
Clearly phony INDIANS dance around her to the beat of DRUMS. The HEROES crawl slowly forward. HICKOK, eyeing the girl lustfully, joins in.)

FIRST LADY. That Hickok's rather handsome, isn't he?
OL' TIME PRESIDENT. I'm watching the girl. Note her legs. How white they are. For an Indian. One can almost see the soft inner flesh of her thighs.
FIRST LADY. *This play excites me*!
OL' TIME PRESIDENT. We really should have more things like this at the White House.

(*The DRUMS grow wilder. The INDIANS scream; BUNTLINE, CODY and HICKOK invade the Indian camp site. GUNSHOTS. INDIANS fall dead.*)

TESKANJAVILA. (*Italian accent.*) Saved! A maiden's prayers are answered! And may I say, not a bit too soon!

Already, my soft thighs had been pried open; my budding breasts pricked by the hot tip of an Indian spear. Yet, through it all, my maidenhead stayed secure. Here. In this pouch. Kept in this secret pocket. Where no one thought to look. Thus is innocence preserved! May Nazuma, God of Thunder, grant me happiness!

(*THUNDER heard.*)

    WILD BILL HICKOK. Buntline write that speech?
    BUFFALO BILL. I think she changed it a little.

(*UNCAS rises from the dead.*)

    UNCAS. (*German accent.*) I am Uncas, Chief of the Pawnee Indians, recently killed for my lustful ways. Yet, before the white men came and did me in, I had this vision: the white man is great, the red man nothing. So, if a white man kills a red man, we must forgive him, for God intended man to be as great as possible, and by eliminating the inferior, the great man carries on God's work. Thus, the Indian is in no way wronged by being murdered. Indeed, quite the opposite: being murdered is his purpose in life. This was my recent vision. Which has brought light to the darkness of my otherwise useless soul ... And now, I die again. (*HE collapses.*)
    WILD BILL HICKOK. Buntline write that?
    BUFFALO BILL. Think Hookman changed it also. They all do it. It's our style. I dunno, people seem to like it.
    WILD BILL HICKOK. Yeah? Well then, guess it mus' be my turn! (*HE pulls out his bowie knife.*)
    BUFFALO BILL. HEY!
    WILD BILL HICKOK. Make one false move an' I'll rip you 'part, friend or no.

BUNTLINE. Bill, look—

WILD BILL HICKOK. As for you, Buntline, you fangless lizard, you harmless bull, you ball of—

BUNTLINE. BRING DOWN THE CURTAIN!

WILD BILL HICKOK. First one touches that curtain, I cuts int' mincemeat an' eats fer dinner, *raw*!

FIRST LADY. I'm trembling all over.

WILD BILL HICKOK. Okay, Buntline. Now we're gonna settle up the score.

BUNTLINE. *Score*?

WILD BILL HICKOK. Men just don' humiliate Wil' Bill Hickok.

BUNTLINE. *Humiliate*?

WILD BILL HICKOK. Or leastways don' do it twice, bein' dead shortly after the first occasion.

BUNTLINE. Wh—what ... 're you talkin' about?

WILD BILL HICKOK. 'Bout havin' to impersonate myself. 'Bout the humiliation o' having' to impersonate my *own personal self*!

BUNTLINE. Oh.

FIRST LADY. *Fantastic*!

BUNTLINE. Well, I dunno what t' say.

WILD BILL HICKOK. It weren't in the deal!

BUNTLINE. Deal?

WILD BILL HICKOK. You said if I came here, I could play Bat Masterson!

BUNTLINE. Ah, *that*! (*HE chuckles.*) Well, ... if you recall, I said *maybe* you could play Bat Masterson. First we had t' see how good you did as Hickok.

WILD BILL HICKOK. As *Hickok*? Chrissake, I AM Hickok!

BUNTLINE. Right.

WILD BILL HICKOK. Well, why in hell should I play *him* then?

BUNTLINE. Well, there's audience appeal.

FIRST LADY. There sure is!

BUNTLINE. BILL! Now—now, wait-a-second! Let's talk this over. Like gentlemen.

BUFFALO BILL. Yeah. Right. Let's ... not get too ... carried away. After all—

WILD BILL HICKOK. If you don' stay out o' this, I'm gonna slit yer stuffin' gizzard an' extract, inch by inch, what's guts in most folks, but in you is thorou' garbage.

BUFFALO BILL. Now wait-a-minute! Hold on! You— you think I'm jus' gonna stand here an'—

WILD BILL HICKOK. Oh, shut up! Dumb, dudelickin' FRAUD!

BUFFALO BILL. *What?*

WILD BILL HICKOK. If I gotta play Hickok, I'm gonna play Hickok the way Hickok should be *played!*

BUNTLINE. *Put that knife away, please!* ... For godsakes. Cody, *HELP ME! Cody!* (*BUNTLINE falls, a knife in his back. HE crawls off the front of the stage; collapses.*)

FIRST LADY. He looks kind o' dead.

(*BUFFALO BILL heads for the body, stunned.*)

WILD BILL HICKOK. Sorry, Will. Guess I just ain't used to show business yet. (*HE chuckles and turns his attention to Teskanjavila.*)

(*BUFFALO BILL is feeling for Buntline's pulse.*)

TESKANJAVILA. O, *Sancta Maria,* I don' like this gleam in his eyes.

WILD BILL HICKOK. (*Striking a pose.*)
Hail, sweet cookie, tart of tempting flavors,
Why've I been denied your spicy favors?

TESKANJAVILA. AH! *What're you doing?* HELP!

(*HICKOK unties her from the pole, at the same time unhooking his gun belt. HE works rapidly.*
BUFFALO BILL lets Buntline's limp arm drop. HE stares back at the stage, stunned.)

FIRST LADY. Ooooh, look what he's doing now!

(*The FIRST FAMILY climb on the stage. The Negro USHERS bringing their chairs for them so they can have a more comfortable view.*)

FIRST LADY. Really, we must invite this theatre crowd more often.

(*HICKOK is now standing above TESKANJAVILA, who lies helplessly at his feet. BUFFALO BILL watches from offstage, outside the ring. Also helpless.*)

WILD BILL HICKOK. Hickok, fastest shooter in the West, 'cept for Billy the Kid, who ain't as accurate; Hickok, deadliest shooter in the West 'cept for Doc Holliday, who wields a sawed-off shotgun, which ain't fair; Hickok, shootinest shooter in the West, 'cept for Jesse James, who's absolutely indiscriminate; this Hickok, strong as an eagle, tall as a mountain, swift as the wind, fierce as a rattlesnake—a legend in his own time, or any other—this Hickok stands now above an Indian maiden—

TESKANJAVILA. I'm not an Indian and I'm not a maiden!

WILD BILL HICKOK. Who's not an Indian and not a maiden, but looks pretty good anyhow—an' asks those o' you watchin' t' note carefully the basic goodness of his very generous intentions, since otherwise ... (*HE starts to finger her clothing.*) ... they might be mistaken for ... (*HE rips open her buckskin dress.*) ... *LUST!*

TESKANJAVILA. (*She is left in a frilly Merry Widow corset.*) Eh, bambino. If you don' mind, I'd like a little privacy. (*To the First Family.*) After all, I've not rehearsed this.

(*HICKOK pulls the cord, lowering the curtain.*)

OL' TIME PRESIDENT. Good show, Cody! *Good show!*

(*BUFFALO BILL, in a daze, walks to the stage and opens the curtain.*
"Scouts of the Plains" drop seen. HE stares at it. Pulls it down. NO ONE THERE.
Mozart MINUET heard.
HE looks around in total confusion. The stage and all the White House furniture begin to disappear.
LIGHTS fade to black, BUFFALO BILL spinning dizzily in the middle.
MUSIC fades.)

Scene 8

LIGHTS up again on the SENATE COMMITTEE.

SENATOR LOGAN. Mister Grass. Let's leave the question of the steamboat. You mentioned the treaty at Fort Lyon and said that parts of that treaty had never been fulfilled. Well, I happen to be quite familiar with that particular treaty and happen to know that it is the Indians who did not fulfill its terms, not us.

JOHN GRASS. We did not *want* the cows you sent!

SENATOR LOGAN. You signed the treaty.

JOHN GRASS. We did not understand that we were to give up part of our reservation in exchange for these cows.

SENATOR DAWES. Why'd you think we were giving you twenty-five thousand cows?

JOHN GRASS. We were hungry. We thought it was for food.

SENATOR LOGAN. It wasn't explained that *only* if you gave us part of your reservation would you receive these cows?

JOHN GRASS. Yes. That was explained.

SENATOR MORGAN. And yet, you thought it was a gift.

JOHN GRASS. Yes.

SENATOR LOGAN. In other words, you thought you could have both the cows and the land?

JOHN GRASS. Yes.

SENATOR DAWES. Even though it was explained that you couldn't.

JOHN GRASS. Yes.

SENATOR MORGAN. This is quite hard to follow.

SENATOR LOGAN. Mister Grass, tell me, which would you prefer, cows or land?

JOHN GRASS. We prefer them both.

SENATOR LOGAN. Well, what if you can't have them both?

JOHN GRASS. We prefer the land.

SENATOR LOGAN. Well then, if you knew you had to give up some land to get these cows, why did you sign the treaty?

JOHN GRASS. The white men made our heads dizzy, and the signing was an accident.

SENATOR LOGAN. An accident?

JOHN GRASS. They talked in a threatening way, and whenever we asked questions, shouted and said we were stupid. Suddenly, the Indians around me rushed up and signed the paper. They were like men stumbling in the dark. I could not catch them.

SENATOR LOGAN. But you signed it, too.

(Long pause.)

SENATOR DAWES. Mister Grass. Tell me. Do the Indians really expect to keep all this land and yet do nothing toward supporting themselves?

JOHN GRASS. We do not have to support ourselves. The Great Father promised to give us everything we ever needed; for that, we gave him the Black Hills.

SENATOR LOGAN. Mister Grass. Which do you prefer—to be self-sufficient or to be given things?

JOHN GRASS. We prefer them both.

SENATOR DAWES. Well, you can't *have* them both!

BUFFALO BILL. *Please!*

JOHN GRASS. I only know what we were promised.

SENATOR DAWES. That's *not* what you were promised!

JOHN GRASS. We believe it is.

BUFFALO BILL. *What's going on here?*

SENATOR MORGAN. Mister Grass. Wouldn't you and your people like to live like the white man?

JOHN GRASS. We are happy like the Indian!

SENATOR LOGAN. He means, you wouldn't like to see your people made *greater*, let's say?

JOHN GRASS. That is not possible! The Cheyenne and the Sioux are as great as people can be, already.

SENATOR MORGAN. Extraordinary, really.

BUFFALO BILL. Mister Grass. Surely, *surely*, your people would like to *improve their condition!*

JOHN GRASS. We would like what is owed us! If the white man want to give us more, that is fine also.

SENATOR LOGAN. Well, we'll see what we can do.

SENATOR MORGAN. Let's call the next. This is getting us nowhere.

JOHN GRASS. We would especially like the money the Great Father says he is holding for us!

SENATOR DAWES. I'm afraid that may be difficult, since, in the past, we've found that when an Indian's been given money, he's spent it all on liquor.

JOHN GRASS. When he's been given money, it's been so little there's been little else he could buy.

SENATOR MORGAN. Whatever, the Great Father does not like his Indian children getting drunk!

JOHN GRASS. Then tell the Great Father, who says he wishes us to live like white men, that when an Indian gets drunk, he is merely imitating the white men he's observed!

(*Laughter from the INDIANS. LOGAN raps his gavel.*)

SENATOR DAWES. STOP IT!

(*No effect. LOGAN raps more.*)

SENATOR DAWES. What in God's name do they think we're doing here? STOP IT!

(*Over the Indians' noise, the noise of a Wild West Show is heard; LIGHTS fade to black.*)

Scene 9

*Wild West Show MUSIC and crisscrossing multicolored
SPOTLIGHTS. The rodeo ring rises from the stage, its
lights glittering. Wild West Show banners descend
above the ring.*

VOICE. And now, ladies and gentlemen, let's hear it for
Buffalo Bill's fantastic company of authentic western
heroes ... the fabulous ROUGHRIDERS OF THE
WORLD!

*(Enter, on heroically artificial horses, the
ROUGHRIDERS—themselves heroically oversized.
THEY gallop about the ring in majestic, intricate
formation, whoopin' and shootin' as they do.)*

VOICE. With the ever-lovely ... ANNIE OAKLEY!

*(ANNIE OAKLEY performs some startling trick shots as
the OTHERS ride in circles about her.)*

VOICE. And now, once again, here he is—the star of
our show, the Ol' Scout himself; I mean the indestructible
and ever-popular—

(DRUM ROLL.)

VOICE. —BUFFALO BILL!

*(Enter, on horseback, BUFFALO BILL. He is in his Wild
West finery.
HE tours the ring in triumph while his ROUGHRIDERS
ride after him, finally exiting to leave him in the center,
alone.)*

BUFFALO BILL. THANK YOU, THANK YOU! A *GREAT* show lined up tonight! With all-time favorite Johnny Baker, Texas Jack and his twelve-string guitar, the Dancin' Cavanaughs, Sheriff Brad and the Deadwood Mail Coach, Harry Philamee's Trained Prairie Dogs, The Abilene County Girls' School Trick Roping and Lasso Society, Pecos Pete and the—

VOICE. *Bill.*

BUFFALO BILL. (*Startled.*) Hm?

VOICE. Bring on the Indians.

BUFFALO BILL. What?

VOICE. The *Indians.*

BUFFALO BILL. Ah.

(*BUFFALO BILL looks uneasily toward the wings as his company of INDIANS enters solemnly and in ceremonial warpaint; THEY carry the Sun Dance pole. At its summit is a buffalo skull.*)

BUFFALO BILL. And now, while my fabulous company of authentic ... American Indians go through the ceremonial preparations of the Sun Dance, which they will re-create in all its death-defying goriness—let's give a warm welcome back to a courageous warrior, the magnificent Chief Joseph—

(*Some COWBOY ROUSTABOUTS set up an inverted tub; MUSIC for Chief Joseph's entrance.*)

BUFFALO BILL. —who will recite his ... celebrated speech. CHIEF JOSEPH!

(*Enter CHIEF JOSEPH, old and hardly able to walk.*)

CHIEF JOSEPH. In the moon of the cherries blossoming, in the year of our surrender, I, Chief Joseph, and what remained of my people, the Nez Percés, were sent to a prison in Oklahoma, though General Howard had promised we could return to Idaho, where we'd always lived. In the moon of the leaves falling, still in the year of our surrender, William Cody came to see me. He was a nice man. With eyes that seemed frightened; I don't know why. He told me I was courageous and said he admired me. Then he explained all about his Wild West Show, in which the great Sitting Bull appeared, and said if I agreed to join, he would have me released from prison, and see that my people received food. I asked what I could do, as I was not a very good rider or marksman. And he looked away and said, "Just repeat, twice a day, three times on Sundays, what you said that afternoon when our army caught you at the Canadian border, where you'd been heading, and where you and your people would have all been safe." So I agreed. For the benefit of my people.... And for the next year, twice a day, three times on Sundays, said this to those sitting around me in the dark, where I could not see them, a light shining so brightly in my eyes! (*Pause. HE climbs up on the tub. Accompanied by exaggerated and inappropriate gestures.*) "Tell General Howard I know his heart. I am tired of fighting. Our chiefs have been killed. Looking Glass is dead. The old men are all dead. It is cold and we have no blankets. The children are freezing. My people, some of them, have fled to the hills and have no food or warm clothing. No one knows where they are—perhaps frozen. I want to have time to look for my children and see how many of them I can find. Maybe I shall find them among the dead. Hear me, my chiefs. I am tired. My heart is sick and sad. From where the sun now stands, I will fight no more forever ...." (*HE climbs down from the tub.*)

After which, the audience always applauded me. (*Exit CHIEF JOSEPH.*)

(*Pause.*)

BUFFALO BILL. The Sun Dance ... was the one religious ceremony common to all the tribes of the plains—the Sioux, the Crow, the Blackfeet, the Kiowa, the Blood, the Cree, the Chippewa, the Arapaho, the Pawnee, the Cheyenne. It was *their* way of proving they were ... real Indians. (*Pause.*) The bravest would take the ends of long leather thongs and hook them through their chest muscles, then, pull till they'd ripped them out. The greater the pain they could endure, the greater they felt the Spirits would favor them. Give them what they needed ... Grant them ... salvation. (*Pause.*) Since the Government has officially outlawed this ritual, we will merely imitate it. (*Pause.*) And no one ... will be hurt. (*HE steps back.*)

(*The dance begins. The INDIANS take the barbed ends of long leather thongs that dangle from the top of the Sun Dance pole and hook them through plainly visible chest harnesses. Then THEY pull back against the center and dance about it, flailing their arms and moaning as if in great pain.*
Suddenly JOHN GRASS enters. A ROUSTABOUT tries to stop him.
The INDIANS are astonished to see this intruder; BUFFALO BILL stunned.
JOHN GRASS pulls the Indians out of their harnesses, rips open his shirt, and sticks the barbs through his chest muscles. HE chants and dances. The other INDIANS, realizing what he's doing, blow on reed whistles, urging him on. Finally HE collapses, blood pouring from his chest.

The INDIANS gather around him in awe.
BUFFALO BILL walks slowly toward John Grass; stares
   down at him.
The INDIANS remove the Sun Dance pole and trappings.
BUFFALO BILL crouches and cradles John Grass in his
   arms.
As LIGHTS fade to black.)

Scene 10

LIGHT up on White House USHER.

   USHER. The President is exercising in the gym, sir.
This way.
   BUFFALO BILL. (*Enters.*) You're sure it's all right?
   USHER. Yes, sir. He said to show you right in. Very
pleased you're here.

(*The USHER gestures for Cody to pass. When HE does,*
   the USHER bows, turns and leaves.
BUFFALO BILL stops.
GYM NOISE heard.
LIGHTS up on the OL' TIME PRESIDENT, dressed like
   Hickok and astride a mechanical horse pushed by
   another USHER. Near him sits an old Victrola; "On the
   Old Chisholm Trail" is playing.
The OL' TIME PRESIDENT spurs his horse onwards.
Nearby hangs a punching bag.
BUFFALO BILL stares at the scene, stupefied; walks
   cautiously forward.)

   BUFFALO BILL. Uh—

OL' TIME PRESIDENT. *Cody*! My ol' buddy! Welcome back! Long time no see!

BUFFALO BILL. Yes, sir. Long time ... no see.

OL' TIME PRESIDENT. Wha'd'ya think o' this thing? Latest in athletic equipment. Just got it yesterday.

BUFFALO BILL. It's a ... nice imitation.

OL' TIME PRESIDENT. More power.

USHER. Pardon?

OL' TIME PRESIDENT. *Little more power.*

(The USHER nods; the mechanical HORSE bounces faster.)

OL' TIME PRESIDENT. Good for the figure, this bronco riding. GIDDYAP! You orn'ry sonofabitch. (*HE laughs; whips his horse furiously.*)

BUFFALO BILL. Sir. What I've come t' talk t' you about is very important.

OL' TIME PRESIDENT. Can't hear ya. Speak up!

BUFFALO BILL. (*Pointing to the phonograph.*) May I turn this down?

OL' TIME PRESIDENT. Tell me. You think I look a little bit like Hickok?

BUFFALO BILL. Mr. President would you *please stop this*?

OL' TIME PRESIDENT. What?

BUFFALO BILL. *STOP THIS!!!*

OL' TIME PRESIDENT. Whoa, Nellie.

USHER. Pardon?

OL' TIME PRESIDENT. WHOA, NELLIE!

(The USHER stops the horse; shuts off the phonograph. Cold tone.)

OL' TIME PRESIDENT. All right. What is it?

BUFFALO BILL. Well sir, I'm here t'ask if you'd come with me t' Sitting Bull's reservation.

OL' TIME PRESIDENT. *Whose* reservation?

BUFFALO BILL. Sitting Bull's. He was in my Wild West Show for a time. And naturally, I feel a sort of ... obligation. Personal ... obligation.

OL' TIME PRESIDENT. I see.

BUFFALO BILL. *I* figure you're just about the only one left now who can really help him. His people are in a desperate way.

OL' TIME PRESIDENT. Tell me: this—uh—Sitting Bull. Isn't he the one who wiped out Custer?

BUFFALO BILL. Uh, well, yes, he ... is, but it was, ya know, nothin'—uh—personal. (*Weak laugh.*)

OL' TIME PRESIDENT. Can't help.

BUFFALO BILL. What?

OL' TIME PRESIDENT. I'm sorry, but I can't help.

BUFFALO BILL. *You don't understand* the *situation*!

OL' TIME PRESIDENT. I *don't*? All right, let's say I *want* to help. *What do I do for 'em*? Do I give 'em back their land? Do I resurrect the buffalo?

BUFFALO BILL. You can do *other* things!

OL' TIME PRESIDENT. No, Cody. *Other* People can do other things. *I* ... must do magic. Well, I can't *do* magic for *them;* it's too late.

BUFFALO BILL. I promised Sitting Bull you'd come.

OL' TIME PRESIDENT. Then you're a fool

BUFFALO BILL. They're going to *die.*

(*Long pause.*)

OL' TIME PRESIDENT. Tell ya what. 'Cause I'm so *grateful* to you .... For your Wild West Show. For what's it's *done*. For this country's *pride*, its *glory*. (*Pause.*) I'll do you a favor; I'll send a committee in my place.

BUFFALO BILL. A committee *won't be able to help*!

OL' TIME PRESIDENT. Oh, I think the gesture will mean something.

BUFFALO BILL. *To WHOM*?

(*Silence.*)

OL' TIME PRESIDENT. Being a great President, Cody, is like being a great eagle. A great ... *hunted* eagle. I mean, you've got to know *when t' stay put.* (*HE smiles.*) On your way out, Bill, tell the guards, no more visitors today, hm?

(*HE nods to the USHER, who starts to rock him again.*
As BUFFALO BILL slowly leaves.
MUSIC back up.
LIGHTS fade to black.)

Scene 11

LIGHTS up on reservation, as when last seen
The INDIANS are laughing; the SENATORS, rapping for
* silence*

SENATOR DAWES. What in God's name do they think we're doing here?

BUFFALO BILL. (*To Sitting Bull.*) Please! You must tell them to stop this *noise*!

SITTING BULL. You told us you would bring the Great Father.

BUFFALO BILL. I told you! He couldn't come! It's not my fault! Besides, these men are the Great Father's representatives! Talking to them is like talking to him!

SITTING BULL. If the Great Father wants us to believe he is wise, why does he send us men who are stupid?

BUFFALO BILL. They're *not* stupid! They just don't see things the way *you* do!

SITTING BULL. Yes. Because they are stupid.

BUFFALO BILL. They're *not stupid*!

SITTING BULL. Then they must be blind. It is the only other explanation.

BUFFALO BILL. All right. Tell me. Do *you* understand them?

SITTING BULL. Why should I want to understand men who are stupid?

BUFFALO BILL. Because if you *don't,* your people will *starve to death.* (*Long pause.*) All right ... Now. Let me try to explain some ... *basics.* (*To the Senators.*) Well, as you've just seen, the Indian can be hard t' figure. What's one thing t' us is another t' him. For example, farmin'. Now the *real* problem here is not poor soil. The real problem's plowin'. Ya see, the Indian believes the earth is sacred and sees plowin' as a sacrilegious act. Well, if ya can't get 'em t' plow, how can ya teach 'em farmin'? Impossible. Fertile land's another problem. There just ain't much of it, an' what there is, the Indians prefer to use for pony racin'. Naturally, it's been explained to 'em how people can race ponies anywhere, but they *prefer* the fertile land. They say, if their ancestors raced ponies there, that's where *they* must race.... Another difficult problem is land itself. The majority of 'em, ya see, don't understand how land can be owned, since they believe the land was made by the Great Spirits for the benefit of everyone. So, when we do buy land from 'em, they think it's just some kind o' temporary loan, an' figure we're kind o' foolish fer payin' good money for it, much as someone'd seem downright foolish t' us who paid money fer the sky, say, or the ocean. Which ... causes problems. (*Pause.*) Well, what I'm gettin' at is *this*: if *their* way o' seein' is hard fer *us* t' follow, ours is just as hard fer *them*.... There's an old Indian legend that when the first white man arrived, he asked some Indians for enough land t' put his blanket down onto fer the night. So they said yes. An' next thing they knew, he'd unraveled this blanket till it was one long piece o'thread. Then he laid out the thread, an' when he was done, he'd roped off a couple o' square miles. Well, the Indian finds that sort o' behavior hard t' understand. That's all I have t' say. Maybe, if you think about it, some good'll finally come from all this. I dunno.

SENATOR MORGAN. Thank you. We *shall* think about it. And hope the Indians think about it, too. And cause no more disturbances like the one just now.... Ask Sitting Bull if he has anything to say.

BUFFALO BILL. Sitting Bull.

SITTING BULL. Of course I will speak if they desire me to. I suppose it is only such men as they desire who may say anything.

SENATOR LOGAN. Anyone here may speak. If you have something to say, we will listen. Otherwise, sit down.

SITTING BULL. Tell me, do you know who I am, that you talk as you do?

BUFFALO BILL. SITTING BULL, PLEASE!

(*Long Pause.*)

SITTING BULL. I wish to say that I fear I spoke hastily just now. In calling you ... stupid. For my friend William Cody tells me you are here with good intentions. So I ask forgiveness for my unthinking words, which might have caused you to wreak vengeance on my people for what was not their doing, but *mine, alone*.

SENATOR LOGAN. We are pleased you speak so ... sensibly. You are forgiven.

SITTING BULL. I shall tell you, then, what I want you to say to the Great Father for me. And I shall tell you everything that is in my heart. For I know the Great Spirits are looking down on me today and want me to tell you everything that is in my heart. For you are the only people now who can help us. (*Pause.*) My children ... are dying. The have no warm clothes, and their food is gone. The old way is gone. No longer can they follow the buffalo and live where they wish. I have prayed to the Great Spirits to send us back the buffalo, but I have not yet seen any buffalo returning. So I know the old way is gone. I think ... my children must learn a *new* way if they are to live. Therefore, tell the Great Father that if he wishes us to live like white men, we will do so.

(*Stunned reaction from his INDIANS. HE silences then with a wave of his hand.*)

SITTING BULL. For I know that if that pleases him, we will benefit. I am looking always to the benefit of my children, and so, want only to please the Great Father .... Therefore, tell him for me that I have never yet seen a white man starving, so he should send us food so we can live like the white man, as he wants. Tell him, also, we'd like some healthy cattle to butcher—I wish to kill three hundred head at a time. For that is the way the white man lives, and we want to please the Great Father and live the same way. Also, ask him to send us each six teams of mules, because that is the way the white men make a living, and I want my children to make as good a living. I ask for these things only because I was advised to follow your ways. I do not ask for anything that is not needed. Therefore, tell him to send to each person here a horse and buggy. And four yokes of oxen and a wagon to haul wood in, since I have never yet seen a white man dragging wood by hand. Also, hogs, male and female, and male and female sheep for my children to raise from. If I leave anything out in the way of animals that the white men have, it is a mistake, for I want every one of them! For we are great Indians, and therefore should be no less great as white men .... Furthermore, tell him to send us warm clothing. And glass for the windows. And toilets. And clean water. And beds, and blankets, and pillows. And fur coats, and gloves. And hats. And *pretty silk ties*. As you see, I do not ask for anything that is not needed. For the Great Father has advised us to live like white men, so clearly, this is how we should live. For it is your doing that we are here on this reservation, and it is not right for us to live in poverty. And be treated like beasts .... That is all I have to say.

SENATOR LOGAN. I want to say something to that man before he sits down, and I want all the Indians to listen very carefully to what I'm going to tell him .... Sitting Bull, this committee invited you to come here for a friendly talk. When you talked, however, you insulted them. I understand this is not the first time you have been guilty of such an offense.

SITTING BULL. Do you know who I am that you talk the way you do?

SENATOR LOGAN. I know you are Sitting Bull.

SITTING BULL. Do you really not recognize me? Do you really not know who I am?

SENATOR LOGAN. *I said, I know you are Sitting Bull*!

SITTING BULL. You know I am Sitting Bull. But do you know what *position* I hold?

SENATOR DAWES. We do not recognize any difference between you and other Indians.

SITTING BULL. Then I will tell you the difference. So you will never ever make this mistake again. I am here by the will of the Great Spirits, and by their will I am chief. My heart is red and sweet, and I know it is sweet, for whatever I pass near tries to touch me with its tongue, as the bear tastes honey and the green leaves lick the sky. If the Great Spirits have chosen anyone to be leader of their country, know that it is not the Great Father; *it is myself.*

SENATOR DAWES. WHO IS THIS CREATURE?

SITTING BULL. I will show you.

(HE raises his hand. The INDIANS turn and start to leave.)

SENATOR LOGAN. Just a minute, Sitting Bull!

(SITTING BULL stops.)

SENATOR LOGAN. Let's get something straight. You said to this committee that you were chief of all the people of this country and that you were appointed chief by the Great Spirits. Well, I want to say that you were *not* appointed by the Great Spirits. Appointments are not made that way. Furthermore, I want to say that you are arrogant and stupidly proud, for you are not a great chief of this country or any other; that you have no following, no power, no control, and no right to any control.

SITTING BULL. I wish to say a word about my not being a chief, having no authority, being proud—

SENATOR LOGAN. You are on an Indian reservation merely at the sufferance of the Government. You are fed by the Government, clothed by the Government; your children are educated by the Government, and all you have and are today is because of the Government. I merely say these things to notify you that you cannot insult the people of the United States of America or its committees. And I want to say to the rest of you that you must learn that you are the equals of other men and must not let this one man lead you astray. You must stand up to him and not permit him to insult people who have come all this way just to help you.... That is all I have to say.

SITTING BULL. I wish to say a word about my not being a chief, having no authority, being proud, and considering myself a great man in general.

SENATOR LOGAN. We do not care to talk with you any more today.

SENATOR DAWES. Next Indian.

SITTING BULL. I said, I wish to speak about my having no authority, being not a chief, and—

SENATOR LOGAN. I said, we've heard enough of you today!

(*SITTING BULL raises his hand; the INDIANS leave.*)

SITTING BULL. (*Stares at Cody.*) If a man is the chief of a great people, and has lived only for those people, and has done many great things for them, *of course he should be proud!* (*He exits.*)

(*LIGHTS fade to black.*)

Scene 12

Guitar heard: "Chisholm Trail."
LIGHTS up on saloon. Most of it is in shadows. Only a
*   poker table is well lit.*
A bar in the distance.
Swinging doors.
Various COWBOYS slouch about.

JESSE JAMES. (*Sings.*)
Walkin' down the street in ol' Dodge City,
Wherever I look things look pretty shitty.
Coma ti yi youpy, youpy yea, youpy yea,
Coma ti yi youpy, youpy yea.
An' the very worst thing that I can see,
Is a dead man walkin' straight toward me.
Coma ti yi youpy, youpy yea, youpy yea,
Coma ti yi youpy, youpy yea.
This dead man clearly ain't feelin' well,
If you ask me I think he's just found hell.
Coma ti yi youpy, youpy yea, youpy yea,
Coma ti yi youpy, you—

(*Enter BUFFALO BILL in an overcoat flecked with snow.
Gloves. A warm scarf.*)

BUFFALO BILL. Where's Hickok? I'm told Hickok's
here .... *Where's Hickok?*
BILLY THE KID. Hey, uh ... stranger.

(*HE chuckles. Before he can draw BUFFALO BILL gets
the drop on him.*)

BUFFALO BILL. Who're you?
PONCHO. He ... is the original ... Billy the Kid.

(*JESSE JAMES makes a move and BUFFALO BILL
draws his other gun; gets the drop on him as well.*)

PONCHO. And *he* is the original Jesse James. The
original Doc Holliday is, I'm afraid, out to lunch.

(*The COWBOYS move to encircle Buffalo Bill.*)

PONCHO. Who're *you*?
BUFFALO BILL. Buffalo Bill.
PONCHO. Really? (*PONCHO laughs.*)
WILD BILL HICKOK.(*Enters.*) Cody! My ol' buddy!

(*THEY embrace.*)

WILD BILL HICKOK. Oh, great balls o'fire! What a surprise! Why jus' this mornin' I was ... was ... (*Pause.*) *picturin'* you.
BUFFALO BILL. You were?
WILD BILL HICKOK. So how ya been? C'mon. Tell me.
BUFFALO BILL. Oh, I been ... fine.
WILD BILL HICKOK. Great!
BUFFALO BILL. An' you?
WILD BILL HICKOK. Never better. *Never better*!
BUFFALO BILL. Mus' say, you've sure got some famous people here. (*Slight laugh.*)
WILD BILL HICKOK. Well, ya know, it's ... that kind o' place. (*HE laughs, too; slaps Cody on the back. HE leads him to a table.*) So! ... Whatcha doin' here? Great honor. *Great honor*!
BUFFALO BILL. I hafta talk t' you.
WILD BILL HICKOK. Sure thing.

(*HE waves the Cowboys away; THEY sit at the table in privacy.*)

BUFFALO BILL. I've just come from Sitting Bull's reservation.
WILD BILL HICKOK. That's a far piece from here.
BUFFALO BILL. I need your help! Sitting Bull is ...

(*Pause.*)

WILD BILL HICKOK. What?

(*Long silence.*)

BUFFALO BILL. I'm scared I dunno what's happenin' anymore .... Things have gotten *beyond* me. (*HE takes a drink.*) I see them *everywhere.* (*Weak smile; almost a laugh.*)

(*MUSIC.*
INDIANS appear in the shadows beyond the saloon.)

BUFFALO BILL. In the grass. The rocks. The branches of dead trees. (*Pause.*) Took a drink from a river yesterday an' they were even there, beneath the water, their hands reachin' up, I dunno whether beggin', or t' ... drag me under. (*Pause.*) I wiped out their food, ya see .... Didn't *mean* to, o' course. (*HE laughs to himself.*) I mean IT WASN'T MY FAULT! The railroad men needed food. They *hired* me t' *find* 'em food! How was *I* t' know the goddam buffalo reproduced so slowly? *How was I t' know that*? NO ONE KNEW THAT!

(*Pause. The INDIANS slowly disappear.*)

BUFFALO BILL. Now, Sitting Bull is ...

(*Long pause.*)

WILD BILL HICKOK. *What*?
BUFFALO BILL. The ... hearing was a shambles. I brought these Senators, you see. To Sitting Bull's reservation. It was a shambles. (*Pause.*) So we left. He *insulted* them. (*Pause.*) Then I saw the letter.

(*Silence.*)

WILD BILL HICKOK. What letter?

BUFFALO BILL. The letter to McLaughlin. The letter ordering it to be ... done. (*Pause.*) So I rode back. Rode all night. Figuring, maybe if I can just *warn* him ... But the reservation soldiers stopped me and made me drink with them. And by the time I got there, he ... was dead. The greatest Indian who'd ever lived. Shot. By order of the Government. Shot with a Gatling gun. (*Pause.*) While the wonderful, gray horse I'd given him for ... appearing in my show danced his repertory of tricks in the background. Since a gunshot was his cue to perform. (*HE laughs. Stops. Long silence.*)

WILD BILL HICKOK. Well now. In exactly what way did you imagine *I* could *help* this situation?

BUFFALO BILL. You have what I *need* ... now.

WILD BILL HICKOK. (*Smiling slightly.*) Oh?

BUFFALO BILL. I'm *scared*, you see. (*Pause.*) Scared ... not so much of *dyin'*, but dyin' *wrong*. (*Slight laugh.*) Dyin' in the center of my arena with ... makeup on. (*Long pause.*) Then I thought of you ... Remembered that night in the White House. Remembered thinking, "My God! Look at Hickok. Hickok *knows just who he is*!" (*Pause.*) "*Hickok has the answer*," I said ... Hickok knows who he *is*. (*Pause.*) I must see Hickok again.

(*Long silence.*)

WILD BILL HICKOK. Well I'm glad you came. Yes. Glad to be able to help. (*Pause.*) Funny. That night in the White House, I remember thinking: "My God, it's *Cody* who's got the answer!"

BUFFALO BILL. ... What?

WILD BILL HICKOK. Poncho!

PONCHO. *Si, señor*.

WILD BILL HICKOK. Bring in our ... um ...

PONCHO. Ah! *Si, señor! Ahorita*. (*Exit PONCHO*.)

WILD BILL HICKOK. Naturally, at first, you may be a bit startled. Put off. Not ... exactly what you *had in mind*. Yet! I'm sure that once you *think* about it, you'll agree *it's the only way*. Just like Jesse has. Billy. Doc Holliday. The boys.

BUFFALO BILL. *What are you talkin' about*?

WILD BILL HICKOK. Why, takin' what you were and raisin' it to a higher level. (*HE laughs*.) Naturally, for my services, I get a small fee. Percentage. You get fifty percent right off the top. Of course, if at any time you aren't happy, you can leave. Take your business elsewhere. That's written in. Keeps us on our toes. Mind you, this enterprise .is still in its infancy. The *potential*, though is unlimited. For example, think of this. The *great national good* ... that could come from this: some of you, let's say, would concentrate strictly on theatrics. MEANWHILE! *Others* of you would concentrate on purely humanitarian affairs. Save ... well, not Sitting Bull, but ... some Indian down in Florida. Another up in Michigan. Perhaps expand into Canada. Mexico. Central America. SOUTH AMERICA! My God, there must be literally *millions* of people who could benefit by your presence! Your ... *simultaneous presence*!

PONCHO. Here they are, *señor*!

(*Enter a group of MEN dressed as Buffalo Bill. Their faces are covered by masks of his face. They wear his florid buckskin clothes—if anything, even more elaborately designed.*)

WILD BILL HICKOK. Naturally, we've still got a few wrinkles to iron out. Color of hair. Color of eyes. That sort of thing. But with *you* here, exercising artistic control, why, we could go on like this *forever*!

(*BUFFALO BILL, stunned by the sight, fires his guns at the duplicate Codys. THEY fall and immediately rise again.*
THEY slowly surround him.
HE screams as HE shoots.
THEY disappear.
The saloon fades to black.)

BUFFALO BILL. (*Alone on stage.*) AND NOW TO CLOSE! AND *NOW TO CLOSE*!
VOICE. Not yet. (*Pause.*) They also killed the rest of his tribe.

(*MUSIC.*
INDIANS enter mournfully. THEY carry a large white sheet.
Sound of WIND.
BUFFALO BILL watches, then moves slowly away; exits.)

Scene 13

The INDIANS cover the center area with the huge white sheet, then lie down upon it in piles.
Enter COLONEL FORSYTH, a LIEUTENANT, and two REPORTERS, their coat collars turned up for the wind. CODY is with them; HE carries a satchel.

FIRST REPORTER. Fine time of year you men picked for this thing.

COLONEL FORSYTH. They're heathens; they don't celebrate Christmas.

FIRST REPORTER. I don't mean the date, I mean the weather.

COLONEL. Uncomfortable?

FIRST REPORTER. Aren't you?

COLONEL. One gets used to it.

SECOND REPORTER. Colonel, I gather we lost twenty-nine men, thirty-three wounded. How many Indians were killed?

COLONEL. We wiped them out.

SECOND REPORTER. Yes, I know. But how many *is* that?

COLONEL. We haven't counted.

LIEUTENANT. The snow has made it difficult. It started falling right after the battle. The bodies were covered almost at once. By night they were frozen.

COLONEL. We more than made up for Custer, though, I can tell you that.

SECOND REPORTER. But Custer was killed fifteen years ago!

COLONEL. So what?

LIEUTENANT. If there are no more questions, we'll take you to—

FIRST REPORTER. I have one! Colonel Forsyth, some people are referring to your victory yesterday as a massacre. How do you feel about that?

COLONEL. One can always find someone who'll call an overwhelming victory a massacre. I suppose they'd prefer it if we'd let more of our own boys get shot!

FIRST REPORTER. Then you don't think the step you took was harsh?

COLONEL. Of course it was harsh. And I don't like it any more than you. But had we shirked our responsibility, skirmishes would have gone on for years, costing our country millions, as well as untold lives. Of course innocent people have been killed. In war they always are. And of course our hearts go out to the innocent victims of this. But war is not a game. It's tough. And demands tough decisions. In the long run I believe what happened here at this reservation yesterday will be justified.

FIRST REPORTER. Are you implying that the Indian Wars are finally over?

COLONEL. Yes, I believe they're finally over. This ludicrous buffalo religion of Sitting Bull's people was their last straw.

SECOND REPORTER. And now?

COLONEL. The difficult job of rehabilitating begins. But that's more up General Howard's line.

LIEUTENANT. Why don't we go and talk with him? He's in the temporary barracks.

COLONEL. He can tell you about our future plans.

(*THEY start to leave.*)

BUFFALO BILL. You said you'd—

LIEUTENANT. Ah, yes, it's that one. (*HE points to a body.*)

BUFFALO BILL. Thank you.

(*HE stays. The OTHERS leave; HE stares at the grave. SITTING BULL has entered, unnoticed. BUFFALO BILL takes a sprig of pine from the satchel and is about to put it on the grave.*)

SITTING BULL. Wrong grave. I'm over here ... As you see, the dead can be buried, but not so easily gotten rid of.

BUFFALO BILL. Why didn't you listen to me? I *warned* you what would happen! Why didn't you *listen*?

(*Long silence.*)

SITTING BULL. We had land. You wanted it; you took it. That I understand perfectly. What I cannot understand is why you did all this, *and at the same time* ... professed your love.

(*Pause.*)

BUFFALO BILL. Well ... well, what about *your* mistakes? *Hm*? For, for example: you were very unrealistic ... about things. For ... example: did you *really* believe the buffalo would return? *Magically* return?

SITTING BULL. It seemed no less likely than Christ's returning, and a great deal more useful. Though when I think of their reception here, I can't see why either would really want to come back.

(*Pause.*)

BUFFALO BILL. For awhile, I actually thought my Wild West Show would *help*. I could give you money. Food. Clothing. And also make people *understand* things ... better. (*HE laughs to himself.*) That was my reasoning. Or, anyway, *part* ... of my reasoning.

SITTING BULL. (*Slight smile.*) Your show was very popular.

(*Pause.*)

BUFFALO BILL. We had ... *fun,* though, you and I. (*Pause.*) Didn't we?

SITTING BULL. Oh, yes. And that's the terrible thing. We had all surrendered. We were on reservations. We could not fight, or hunt. We could do nothing. Then you came and allowed us to imitate our glory. It was humiliating! For sometimes, we could almost imagine it was *real.*

BUFFALO BILL. Guess it wasn't so authentic, was it? (*HE laughs slightly to himself.*)

SITTING BULL. How could it have been? You'd have killed all your performed in one afternoon.

(*Pause.*)

BUFFALO BILL. You know what worried me most? ... The fear that I might die, in the middle of the arena, with all my makeup on. *That* ... is what worried me most.

SITTING BULL. What worried *me* most ... was something I'd said the year before. Without thinking.

BUFFALO BILL. What?

SITTING BULL. I'd agreed to go onto the reservation. I was standing in front of my tribe, the soldiers leading us into the fort. And as we walked, I turned to my son, who was beside me. "Now," I said, "you will never know what it is to be an Indian, for you will never again have a gun or pony ... " Only later did I *realize* what I'd said. These things, the gun and the pony—they came with you. And then I thought, ah, how terrible it would be if we finally owe to the white man not only our destruction, but also our glory ... Farewell, Cody. You were my friend. And, indeed you still are ... I never killed you because I *knew it would not matter.* (*HE starts to leave.*)

BUFFALO BILL. If only I could have saved *your* life!

(*SITTING BULL stops and stares at him coldly; turns and leaves. Long pause.*)

BUFFALO BILL. Well! This is it! (*HE forces a weak laugh.*) Naturally, I've been thinking 'bout this moment for quite some time now. As any performer would.

VOICE. And now to close!

BUFFALO BILL. NOT YET! ... I would ... first ... like to ... say a few words in defense of my country's Indian policy, which seems, in certain circles, to be meeting with considerable disapproval. (*HE smiles weakly, clears his throat, reaches into his pocket, draws out some notes, and puts on a pair of eyeglasses.*) The—uh—State of Georgia, anxious to solidify its boundaries and acquire certain valuable mineral rights, hitherto held accidentally by the Cherokee Indians, and anxious, furthermore, to end the seemingly inevitable hostilities between its residents and these Indians on the question of land ownership, initiated, last year, the forced removal of the Cherokee nation, resettling them in a lovely and relatively unsettled area west of the Mississippi known as the Mojave Desert. Given proper irrigation, this spacious place should soon be blooming. Reports that the Cherokees were unhappy at their removal are decidedly untrue. And though many, naturally, died while marching from Georgia to the Mojave Desert, the ones who did, I'm told, were rather ill already, and nothing short of medication could have saved them. Indeed, in all ways, our vast country is speedily being opened for settlement. The shipment of smallpox-infested blankets, sent by the Red Cross to the Mandan Indians, has, I'm pleased to say, worked wonders, and the Mandans are no more. Also, the Government policy of exterminating the buffalo, a policy with which I myself was intimately connected, has practically reached fruition. Almost no buffalo are now left, and soon the Indians will be hungry enough to begin farming in earnest, a step we believe necessary if they are ever to leave their barbaric ways and enter civilization. Indeed, it is for this very reason that we have begun giving rifles to the Indians as part of each treaty with them, for without armaments they could not hope to wage war with us, and the process of civilizing them would be seriously hampered in every way. Another aspect of our benevolent attitude toward these savages is shown by the Government's policy of having its official interpreters translate everything incorrectly when interpreting for the Indians, thereby angering the Indians and forcing them to learn English for themselves. Which, of course, is the first step in civilizing people. I'm reminded here of a story told me by a munitions manufacturer. It seems, by *accident*, he sent a shipment of blank bullets to the Kickapoo Indians, and ... (*HE looks around.*) Well, I won't tell it. It's too involved. I would just like to say that I am sick and tired of these sentimental humanitarians who take no account of the difficulties under which this Government has labored in its efforts to deal fairly with the Indian, nor of the countless lives we have lost and atrocities endured at their savage hands. I quote General Sheridan:—

(*The INDIANS have begun to rise from their graves; for a while THEY stand in silence behind Buffalo Bill, where THEY are joined, at intervals, by the rest of the Indian company.*)

BUFFALO BILL. —"I do not know how far these so-called humanitarians should be excused on account of their political ignorance; but surely it is the only excuse that can give a shadow of justification for their aiding and abetting such horrid crimes as the Indians have perpetrated on our people."

BUFFALO BILL.
The excuse that the Indian way of life is vastly different from ours, and that what seem like atrocities to us do not to them, does not hold water, I'm afraid!

For the truth is, the Indian never had any real title to the soil of this country. We had that title. By *right of discovery*! And all the Indians were, were the temporary occupants *of the land* They *h a d* to be vanquished by us! It was, in fact, our *m o r a l obligation*!

For the earth was given to mankind to support the greatest number of which it is capable; and no tribe or people have a *right* to withhold from the wants of others! For example—

SITTING BULL. (*Very softly*.) I am Sitting Bull—

(*Almost inaudible*.) — and I am—*dying*!

BLACK HAWK.
Black Hawk *is dying*.

TECUMSEH.
Tecumseh *is dying*.
CRAZY   HORSE.
Crazy Horse ... is dying.

RED CLOUD.
Red Cloud *is dying*.

SPOTTED   TAIL.
Spotted Tail ... is dying again.

—in the case of Lone Wolf versus Hitchcock, 1902, the Supreme Court of the United States ruled that the power exists to abrogate the provisions of *any* Indian treaty if the *interests of the country demand*!

SATANTA.
Satanta *is dying*.

Here's another one; in the case of the Seneca Indians versus the Pennsylvania Power Authority, the courts ruled that the Seneca Treaty was invalid since perpetuity was legally a vague phrase. *Vague phrase*! Yes. Ah. Here's one, even better. In the—

KIOKUK.
Kiokuk *is dying*.

GERONIMO.
Geronimo ... *is dying*!

OLD TAZA.
Old Taza *is dying*!

JOHN GRASS.
John Grass is dying.

(*Long pause.*)

No. Wait. Got it. The one I've been looking for. In the case of Sitting Bull versus Buffalo Bill, the Supreme Court ruled that the *inadvertent* slaughter of ... buffalo by ... I'm sorry, I'm ... reminded here of an amusing story told me by General Custer. You remember him—one o' the great dumbass ...

(*The INDIANS begin a soft and mournful moaning.*)

(*Pause.*)

BUFFALO BILL. Think I'd better close. I ... just want to say that anyone who thinks we have done something wrong is *wrong*! And that I have here, in this bag, some— (*HE goes and picks up his satchel; HE looks up and sees the INDIANS staring at him; HE turns quickly away.*)— Indian trinkets. Some ... examples of their excellent workmanship. Moccasins. Beads. Feathered headdresses for your children. (*HE has begun to unpack these trinkets and place them, for display, on a small camp stool he has set across the front edge of the center ring.*) Pretty picture postcards. Tiny Navaho dolls. The money from the sale of these few trifling trinkets will go to help them help themselves. Encourage them a bit. You know, *raise their spirits* ... Ah! Wait. No, sorry, that's a—uh—buffalo skin. (*HE shoves it back in the satchel.*) Yes. Here it is! Look, just look ... at this handsome replica of an ... Indian. Made of genuine wood. (*HE puts the carved head of an Indian on the camp stool so that it overlooks all the other trinkets. The LIGHTS now slowly begin to fade on him; HE sits by the trinkets, trembling.*)

CHIEF JOSEPH. Tell General Howard I know his heart. I am tired of fighting. Our chiefs have been killed. Looking Glass is dead. The old men are all dead. It is cold and we have no blankets. The children are freezing. My people, some of them, have fled to the hills and have no food or warm clothing. No one knows where they are— perhaps frozen. I want to have time to look for my children and see how many of them I can find. Maybe I shall find them among the dead.

(*Almost all the LIGHTS are now gone; CHIEF JOSEPH can hardly be seen; BUFFALO BILL is but a shadow.*

Only the trinkets are clear in a pinspot of LIGHT, and that light, too, is fading.)

CHIEF JOSEPH. Hear me, my chiefs. I am tired. My heart is sick and sad. From where the sun now stands, I will fight no more, forever.

(And then, very slowly, even the LIGHT on the trinkets fades. And the stage is completely dark.
Then, suddenly, all LIGHTS blazing!
Rodeo ring up.
Rodeo MUSIC.
Enter, on horseback, the ROUGHRIDERS of the World. THEY tour the ring triumphantly, then form a line to greet BUFFALO BILL, who enters on his white stallion. HE tours the ring, a glassy smile on his face.
The ROUGHRIDERS exit.
BUFFALO BILL alone, on his horse. HE waves his big Stetson to the unseen crowd.
Then, INDIANS appears from the shadows outside the ring; THEY approach him slowly.
LIGHTS fade to black.
Pause.
LIGHTS return to the way they were at the top of the show, when the audience was entering.
The three glass cases are back in place.
No curtain.)

End of Play

Other Publications for Your Interest

LAKEBOAT
(ADVANCED GROUPS—COMEDY)
By DAVID MAMET

8 men—Unit set

This fascinating series of vignettes, staged to great acclaim by the Milwaukee Repertory Theatre, is set aboard a Great Lakes steamer, bound from Gary to Duluth. It focuses in on the eight-member crew, the hardhats of the steel waterways, all but one of whom are "lifers." The other character is a young college man who has been hired to replace the night cook. He is the closest thing to the central figure. "... the show has much of Mamet's poetry of the inarticulate, the ritual, tribal double-talk that makes sense underneath the ludicrous patters of our lives."—Chicago Tribune. "... a banquet of meaty acting parts."—Milwaukee Sentinel.   (#14017)

GLENGARRY GLEN ROSS
(ADVANCED GROUPS—COMIC DRAMA)
By DAVID MAMET

7 men—2 Interiors

Winner of the London theatre equivalent of our Tony Award, this scalding comedy went on to take Broadway by storm, winning the Pulitzer Prize for drama in 1984. Never has Mr. Mamet's ear for the rhythms of actual, contemporary speech been more keen than in this tale of cutthroat real estate salesmen competing against each other for the money of unwary customers. One suavely vicious salesman, Richard Roma, is in the lead for the monthly sales award: a new Cadillac. Another, Shelly "The Machine" Levene, a former top salesman, is now riding a streak of bad luck on a smile and a shoeshine, hoping to turn his luck around. All are dependent upon an office manager named Williamson to give them the vital "leads" to new customers. Williamson, meanwhile, is pitting them against each other to drive up sales. In the first act, composed of three scenes, we meet the salesmen, vying for position as they gulp their cocktails in the local Chinese restaurant. The second act becomes a sort of "who done it" as the scene shifts to the office, where a burglary has taken place. The vital leads have been filched the night before, possibly by one of the salesmen. In the end, Williamson screws Roma out of his car and nabs the bag man. "Crackling tension . . . ferocious comedy and drama. A top American playwright in bristling form."—N.Y. Times. "Wonderfully funny . . . a play to see, remember and cherish."—N.Y. Post. "Mamet is . . . a pure writer, and the synthesis he appears to be making, with echoes from voices as diverse as Beckett, Pinter and Hemingway, is unique and exciting."—Newsweek.   (#9058)

... for Your Interest

THE BALLAD OF SOAPY SMITH
(ADVANCED GROUPS — EPIC COMIC DRAMA)
By MICHAEL WELLER

...concerned with building elaborate interiors and exteriors (may be unit set)

..."Soapy" Jefferson Randolph Smith, known as "Soapy" to his friends and foes, is a per-
...died notorious con men whose reputation has also, has preceded him to the Alaska
...gold rush town of Skagway, in 1897, when the play takes place. Soapy is a charming
gentleman, and he starts up a protection racket which brings law and order to the town,
giving it a church and an infirmary. Oddly enough Soapy, the criminal, becomes a force for
moral good; until the town's hypocrisy and vicious self interest bring him down, a victim of
the cardinal sin of believing in his own myth... ...or a his-
...tago-
...than
...with
...975)